MW00596444

WALKING TOWARD THE DAWN

Finding Certainty in Our Christian Experience

_____

Jeremiah W. Montgomery

'The path of the righteous is like the light of dawn,
which shines brighter and brighter until full day,'
(Prov. 4:18)

THE BANNER OF TRUTH TRUST

THE BANNER OF TRUTH TRUST

Head Office
3 Murrayfield Road
Edinburgh, EH12 6EL
UK

North America Office
PO Box 621
Carlisle, PA 17013
USA

banneroftruth.org

© The Banner of Truth Trust 2021
First published 2021

*

Print: 978 1 80040 026 9
Epub: 978 1 80040 027 6
Kindle: 978 1 80040 028 3

*

Printed in the USA by
Versa Press Inc.,
East Peoria, IL.

Introduction

NOT ALL WHO WANDER ARE LOST

*The LORD your God is in your midst, a mighty one who will save;
he will rejoice over you with gladness; he will quiet you by his love;
he will exult over you with loud singing.*
(Zephaniah 3:17)

Even for believers, it can be hard to believe the gospel. I read the words of Zephaniah, and I marvel. Imagine it! The everlasting, ever-flowing, ever-glowing fountain of joy, rejoicing over *you*. The voice that spoke the stars into being, singing over *me*. I marvel at the love of God. Yet I also wonder: How can I be sure such wondrous love as this truly rests on me?

I grew up in a Christian home, and I do not know the date of my conversion. Over the course of my life, my Christian upbringing has been a source of so many significant blessings. But in my case, as in the case of others, it has also raised a very serious question: How do I know that Christian experience is real *within* me, and not just *around* me?

For more than twenty-five years, I have walked through the valley of the shadow of doubt, haunted by two things. The first is the fact that since childhood I have prayed to Jesus Christ with the honest desire to be saved. In light of this reality, the second is all the more puzzling, namely that since my teenage years I have struggled to find certainty about my relationship to Jesus Christ.

I am now convinced that these two facts are not that difficult to reconcile. I have indeed known Jesus since childhood; how else could I have called upon his name (Rom. 10:14)? Yet just as a child can spend many years relating to their parents existentially – without understanding who these people really are, and without having any substantial grasp of how relationships actually work – so I have spent many years relating to my Lord in a way that was childish, immature, and uninformed. The result has been a deep, persistent insecurity.

For a long time I did not think there were any clear answers. Then, a little more than a dozen years ago, I received help from a friend which set me on a path out of doubt's shadowed valley. Since that time, through Scripture, through the wisdom of saints past and present, and through many hours of prayerful reflection, the Lord has given me even more lights leading toward the dawn – 'The path of the righteous is like the light of dawn, which shines brighter and brighter until full day' (Prov. 4:18).

The purpose of this booklet is to share these lights, in order that others may draw nearer to a full assurance of the reality of their Christian faith and salvation. For those who are not struggling with doubt, my hope is that this booklet may prove to be preventative medicine that will fortify them against future infection. For those who are wrestling with doubts, my prayer is that this booklet may guide them out of the gloom and into the dawn.

Is such full assurance really possible? The eighteenth chapter of the *Westminster Confession of Faith* teaches us that it is:

> 1. Although hypocrites and other unregenerate men may vainly deceive themselves with false hopes and carnal presumptions of being in the favour of God, and estate of salvation (which hope of theirs shall perish): yet such as truly believe in the Lord Jesus, and love him in sincerity, endeavouring to walk in all good conscience before him, may, in this life, be certainly assured that

they are in the state of grace, and may rejoice in the hope of the glory of God, which hope shall never make them ashamed.

2. This certainty is not a bare conjectural and probable persuasion grounded upon a fallible hope; but an infallible assurance of faith founded upon the divine truth of the promises of salvation, the inward evidence of those graces unto which these promises are made, the testimony of the Spirit of adoption witnessing with our spirits that we are the children of God, which Spirit is the earnest of our inheritance, whereby we are sealed to the day of redemption.

3. This infallible assurance doth not so belong to the essence of faith, but that a true believer may wait long, and conflict with many difficulties before he be partaker of it: yet, being enabled by the Spirit to know the things which are freely given him of God, he may, without extraordinary revelation, in the right use of ordinary means, attain thereunto. And therefore it is the duty of everyone to give all diligence to make his calling and election sure, that thereby his heart may be enlarged in peace and joy in the Holy Ghost, in love and thankfulness to God, and in strength and cheerfulness in the duties of obedience, the proper fruits of this assurance; so far is it from inclining men to looseness.

4. True believers may have the assurance of their salvation divers ways shaken, diminished, and intermitted; as, by negligence in preserving of it, by falling into some special sin which woundeth the conscience and grieveth the Spirit; by some sudden or vehement temptation, by God's withdrawing the light of his countenance, and suffering even such as fear him to walk in darkness and to have no light: yet are they never utterly destitute of that seed of God, and life of faith, that love of Christ and the brethren, that sincerity of heart, and conscience of duty, out of which, by the operation of the Spirit, this assurance may, in due

time, be revived; and by the which, in the meantime, they are supported from utter despair.

The Confession gives us three practical tests. Those who 'truly believe in the Lord Jesus, and love him in sincerity, endeavouring to walk in all good conscience before him, may, in this life, be certainly assured that they are in the state of grace.' Assurance may be reached through a biblical examination of one's faith, one's love, and one's life. The most straightforward of these three tests is the third. A Christian is one who seeks to follow and obey the Lord Jesus Christ in real life. Transformed living is a direct result of a transformed heart: 'If you love me, you will keep my commandments' (John 14:15). If we do not even try to follow Christ, then it is evident that we have no real faith in him. Our lives reflect our Lord. Because this test is the simplest and most obvious, I shall not further unpack it in these pages.

The first and second tests, the questions of our faith and of our love, are more difficult, for the sensitive soul is well aware of its own capacity for hypocrisy. 'The heart is deceitful above all things, and desperately sick; who can understand it?' (Jer. 17:9). In the face of such capacity for self-deception, how do we discern answers to questions of the heart?

Thankfully, the Confession also reminds us that in these matters we have help. Christian certainty is not an educated guess, 'not a bare conjectural and probable persuasion grounded upon a fallible hope.' Rather, we have sure, solid assistance from 'the divine truth of the promises of salvation, the inward evidence of those graces unto which these promises are made, [and] the testimony of the Spirit of adoption witnessing with our spirits that we are the children of God.'

Both the Confession and experience suggest to me that Christian certainty requires two things: sound theological instruction and clear practical guidance. The following material contains both. First, there are five theological truths that provide a foundation for assurance. Following this, there are three practical steps intended to activate these truths.

Let us go forth in hope. Assurance of salvation 'doth not so belong to the essence of faith, but that a true believer may wait long, and conflict with many difficulties before he be partaker of it.' To experience doubt does not mean that one is damned. Moreover, 'being enabled by the Spirit to know the things which are freely given us of God, we may, without extraordinary revelation, in the right use of ordinary means, attain [assurance of salvation].'

One may wander long in the valley of the shadow of doubt. But we need not despair. Not all who wander are lost.

Theological Truth 1

THE FAITHFULNESS OF GOD

God is faithful, by whom you were called into the fellowship of his Son, Jesus Christ our Lord.
(1 Corinthians 1:9)

Finding certainty requires that we begin with a clear understanding of the character of God. The reason for this is simple. Assurance of salvation is 'founded upon the divine truth of the promises of salvation.'[1] Yet a promise is only as good as the one who makes it. If we are to be sure of the promise, we must be sure of the promiser. Therefore, if we want to be sure of our salvation, we must start with accurate ideas about the character of God.

Sadly, this is a trickier business than it ought to be. Ever since the Garden of Eden, we human beings have lived with spiritual poison

[1] *Westminster Confession of Faith*, 18.2.

coursing through our veins. This poison is our pride, the root of every sin. It is an hereditary plague of self-assertion and self-worship, a hell-inspired desire to play god for ourselves.

How did we get this way? Scripture records the fateful event:

> Now the serpent was more crafty than any other beast of the field that the Lord God had made. He said to the woman, 'Did God actually say, "You shall not eat of any tree in the garden"?' And the woman said to the serpent, 'We may eat of the fruit of the trees in the garden, but God said, "You shall not eat of the fruit of the tree that is in the midst of the garden, neither shall you touch it, lest you die."' But the serpent said to the woman, 'You will not surely die. For God knows that when you eat of it your eyes will be opened, and you will be like God, knowing good and evil.' So ... she took of its fruit and ate, and she also gave some to her husband who was with her, and he ate (Gen. 3:1-6).

This passage demonstrates to us the pattern of temptation.[2] First, the command of God is *distorted*. The original command, 'You may surely eat of every tree of the garden, but of the tree of the knowledge of good and evil you shall not eat' (Gen. 2:16, 17), becomes, in the mouth of the serpent, 'You shall not eat of any tree in the garden.' Second, the distorted form of the command is *questioned*: 'Did God actually say ...?' Third, the word of God is *denied*: 'You will not surely die.' Finally, *suspicion* is thrown on God himself: 'For God knows that when you eat of it your eyes will be opened, and you will be like God.'

In deceiving Adam and Eve, the devil achieved his greatest victory. Sinclair Ferguson explains:

---

[2] I am indebted for my understanding of this passage to the insights of Gordon J. Wenham, *Genesis 1-15, Word Biblical Commentary*, Vol. 1 (Grand Rapids: Zondervan, 1987), and Derek Kidner, *Genesis, Tyndale OT Commentaries*, Vol. 1 (Downers Grove, IL: IVP Academic, 2008).

In Eden the Serpent persuaded Eve and Adam that God was possessed of a narrow and restrictive spirit bordering on the malign … What was injected into Eve's mind and affections during the conversation with the Serpent was a deep-seated suspicion of God that was soon further twisted into rebellion against him … what the Serpent accomplished in Eve's mind, affections, and will was a divorce between God's revealed will and his gracious, generous character. Trust in him was transformed into suspicion of him by looking at 'naked law' rather than hearing 'law from the gracious lips of the heavenly Father.' … When this distortion of God's character is complete, we inevitably mistrust him; we lose sight of his love and grace; we see him essentially as a forbidding God.[3]

In aligning with Satan, our first parents swallowed

a lie big enough to reinterpret life … a false system … dynamic enough to redirect the flow of affection and ambition … God will henceforth be regarded, consciously or not, as a rival and enemy … presenting divine love as envy, service as servility, and a suicidal plunge as a leap into life.[4]

This lie has been with us ever since.

What lies at the root of all of humanity's problems? It is *suspicion of God*: the belief that God cannot be trusted. Suspicion of God is what makes us doubt his promises. It is what makes us disbelieve his word and work, whether in history or in our lives. Unless it is removed, it will poison our endeavour. In order to move toward assurance of salvation, we must confess and confront this suspicion of God. Is God a dark monster whom we must either dethrone or escape from? To the contrary:

[3] Sinclair B. Ferguson, *The Whole Christ: Legalism, Antinomianism, and Gospel Assurance – Why the Marrow Controversy Still Matters* (Wheaton, IL: Crossway, 2016), pp. 80-83.
[4] Kidner, *Genesis*, p. 68.

Anyone who does not love does not know God, because God is love. In this the love of God was made manifest among us, that God sent his only Son into the world, so that we might live through him. In this is love, not that we have loved God but that he loved us and sent his Son to be the propitiation for our sins (1 John 4:8-10; see also John 3:16, 17).

The God revealed to us in Scripture is not a demanding tyrant whom we must appease *in order for* him to love us. Christ did not give himself to *make* God love us. Rather, God is a loving Father who gave Christ because he loves us. God is love! We must know this and believe it, not because we always feel it, but because Scripture reveals it.

The loving, trustworthy character of God has an additional implication for our study of assurance. If we commit ourselves to God's revelation of *himself*, we should also commit ourselves to God's word as the standard for evaluating *ourselves*. Feelings of doubt about our salvation may persist for years and may resist all efforts to pin them down. What can we do? We can commit ourselves to the assessment and conclusion of Scripture. On this very point William Guthrie wrote, 'If we prove from Scripture, which is the uncontroverted rule, that you are gracious, and have made a covenant savingly with God, then resolve to grant so much, and to acquiesce in it.'[5]

As we move forward in our pursuit of assurance, let this first light guide our search: all God is, *all God says, and all God does can be trusted, now and forever*. Even when we do not feel this, we may believe it. Let us commit ourselves to believing all God says about himself and about us. At all times and in all things, his verdict can be trusted.

---

[5] William Guthrie, *The Christian's Great Interest* (Edinburgh: Banner of Truth Trust, 2002), p. 26.

Theological Truth 2

THE TRIUMPH OF JESUS

For you know the grace of our Lord Jesus Christ, that though he was rich,
yet for your sake he became poor, so that you
by his poverty might become rich.
(2 Corinthians 8:9)

Having seen what Scripture reveals about the character of God, the second layer of our foundation for assurance is found in the work of Jesus Christ. The apostle Paul writes, 'The saying is trustworthy and deserving of full acceptance, that Christ Jesus came into the world to save sinners, of whom I am the foremost,' (1 Tim. 1:15). But how does Jesus save us? What exactly did he do?

In the fifth chapter of Romans, the apostle explains the work of Christ using the imagery of two men:

> For if, because of one man's trespass, death reigned through that one man, much more will those who receive the abundance of grace and the free gift of righteousness reign in life through the one man Jesus Christ. Therefore, as one trespass led to condemnation for all men, so one act of righteousness leads to justification and life for all men. For as by the one man's disobedience the many were made sinners, so by the one man's obedience the many will be made righteous (Rom. 5:17-19).

The first 'man' mentioned in this passage is Adam, the first human being. The second 'man' is Jesus, whom Paul elsewhere calls 'the last Adam' (1 Cor. 15:45). Each of these men functions like the captain of a team.[6]

---

[6] I am indebted, for this analogy, to Robert Letham, *Union with Christ: in Scripture, History, & Theology* (Phillipsburg, NJ: P&R, 2011), p. 58.

Team captains bear the power and responsibility to make decisions that affect the welfare of others. Every member of the team shares in the outcome of their decisions, whether for good or for evil. Adam's disobedience plunged his team into condemnation. Christ's obedience leads his team into justification and life. By Adam's disobedience, all naturally conceived people 'were made sinners.' By the obedience of Jesus, all supernaturally reborn believers 'will be made righteous.'

It is important to understand that the obedience of Jesus has two sides. Theologians call these two sides his *active* and *passive* obedience. Active obedience refers to Jesus obeying all the positive requirements of God's law. Passive obedience refers to Jesus suffering the full penalty for all our violations of God's law. Christ's obedience was an act of double substitution. 'For our sake he made him to be sin who knew no sin, so that in him we might become the righteousness of God' (2 Cor. 5:21). He did not just *pay* for us; he also *obeyed* for us. If he had done only one, we would have no hope. Think about it. If Jesus paid for your sins, but left it up to you to obey God's commands, could you do it? Jesus himself told us what this would require:

> You shall love the Lord your God with all your heart and with all your soul and with all your mind. This is the great and first commandment. And a second is like it: You shall love your neighbor as yourself. On these two commandments depend all the Law and the Prophets (Matt. 22:37-40).

God's requirement is that we love him completely and perfectly. Even if he were to strip away every other good thing, we are to be content simply to belong to him. We are to love him, not just for his *gifts*, but simply for *himself*.[7] That is the perfection he requires.

---

[7] I am indebted to Tim Keller for this insight. See his excellent discussion of the story of Job in chapter 14, 'Praying,' of Timothy Keller, *Walking With God Through Pain and Suffering* (New York: Dutton, 2013).

Could you or I ever be this perfect, even for a minute, even on our best day? What about on our worst days? For a lifetime? For us, the answer is an unequivocal 'No' (Gal. 5:17; Rom. 7:18). But for Jesus, the answer was an astonishing 'Yes.'

Jesus loved God so much that he laid aside his heavenly glory and entered history as a true and perfect man. Born into a peasant family, he loved God in poverty. Resisting Satan's temptations to take advantage of his divine nature, he loved God in obscurity. Rejected by those who should have received him, he loved God in humility. And finally, bearing the wrath of God against our sins, he loved God in agony. Stripped progressively of every good gift, he persevered in loving God with all his heart, soul, and mind.

Among all the people who have ever lived, Jesus alone loved God perfectly. Even when the greatest blessing – his sense of God's love – was denied him, Jesus yet clung to his Father: 'My God, my God, why have you forsaken me?' (Mark 15:34). 'Skin for skin!' Satan had snarled so long ago. 'All that a man has he will give for his life' (Job 2:4). But Jesus did not just love God to keep his life. Jesus loved God even when it cost him his life.

Why did he do all this? In order to love his neighbour as himself. He lived and died so that we, who deserve wrath, might reign with him forever in life. 'For you know the grace of our Lord Jesus Christ, that though he was rich, yet for your sake he became poor, so that you by his poverty might become rich' (2 Cor. 8:9). The work of Jesus was a perfect triumph. It is historical fact, it is final, and it is fully effective: 'Christ discharged the debt of sin. He bore our sins and purged them. He did not make a token payment which God accepts in place of the whole. Our debts are not cancelled; they are liquidated.'[8]

---

[8] John Murray, *Redemption Accomplished and Applied* (Edinburgh: Banner of Truth Trust, 2016), p. 52. Murray's full discussion of the perfection of Christ's obedience includes its historical objectivity, its finality, its uniqueness, and its effectiveness (see Murray, pp. 45-52).

A struggle with assurance sometimes involves a gap in understanding the obedience of Jesus. Christians are usually familiar with Christ's substitutionary *death*. But we are not always sufficiently mindful of his substitutionary *life*. If we neglect the latter, we may fall into false thinking. We may begin to think that Christ paid the wages of our *sin*, but it remains for us to earn the wages needed to enter *heaven*. Nothing could be farther from the truth of the gospel. We need both active and passive obedience. In Christ we *have* both. As he died, our Lord did not say, 'It is in progress.' Rather, he said, 'It is finished!' (John 19:30).

The work of Jesus lacked nothing and provides everything. As we continue, then, let us remember this second light: *the gospel is not just that Jesus paid for me, but that he also obeyed for me.* He was cursed for me and he is perfect for me.

Theological Truth 3

THE PROMISE OF LIFE

And this is the promise that he made to us – eternal life.
(1 John 2:25)

In one of the most beautiful verses in Scripture, the apostle Paul writes, 'I have been crucified with Christ. It is no longer I who live, but Christ who lives in me. And the life I now live in the flesh I live by faith in the Son of God, who loved me and gave himself for me' (Gal. 2:20). Those of us who struggle with assurance of our salvation long to be able to echo Paul's words. For we believe that he was telling the truth. We believe that Christ loved and gave himself for sinners. But how can we be sure that he 'loved *me* and gave himself for *me*'? This is where we are unsure.

Having considered the character of God and the triumph of Jesus, the third layer of our foundation for assurance is found in the free offer of the gospel. To whom does Jesus offer salvation? Is his promise of forgiveness and eternal life given only to some, or to all? The answer is good news. Though not all will receive him, Jesus offers himself to *all*:

> Come to me, *all* who labor and are heavy laden, and I will give you rest (Matt. 11:28).

> He came to his own, and his own people did not receive him. But to *all* who did receive him, who believed in his name, he gave the right to become children of God, who were born, not of blood nor of the will of the flesh nor of the will of man, but of God (John 1:11-13; see also 3:16; 7:37, 38).

> The Spirit and the Bride say, 'Come.' And let the one who hears say, 'Come.' And let *the one who is thirsty* come; let *the one who desires* take the water of life without price (Rev. 22:17).

The gospel is called 'the promise' repeatedly throughout the New Testament.[9] It is 'the promise of the life that is in Christ Jesus' (2 Tim. 1:1). And it is called 'the promise' at Pentecost:

> Repent and be baptized every one of you in the name of Jesus Christ for the forgiveness of your sins, and you will receive the gift of the Holy Spirit. For the promise is for you and for your children and for all who are far off, everyone whom the Lord our God calls to himself (Acts 2:38, 39).

The gospel does *not* promise universal salvation. However, it *is* a universal promise. The Scottish minister Thomas Boston compared it to a piece of gold offered to a poor man:

---

[9] See Acts 2:39; 26:6; Rom. 4:13, 14, 16, 20; Gal. 3:17, 19, 22; Eph. 3:6; 2 Tim. 1:1; Heb. 11:39, 1 John 2:25.

'That Christ is yours,' viz. by the deed of gift and grant made to mankind lost ... By this offer or deed of gift and grant, Christ is ours before we believe ... Even as when one presents a piece of gold to a poor man saying, 'Take it, it is yours'; the offer makes the piece really his in the sense and to the effect before declared; nevertheless, while the poor man does not accept or receive it; whether apprehending the offer too great to be real, or that he has no liking of the necessary consequents of the accepting; it is not his in possession, nor hath he the benefit of it; but, on the contrary, must starve for it all, and that so much the more miserably, that he hath slighted the offer and refused the gift.[10]

Though the language here is dense, the point is simple: even when it is refused, the gift is real. The same is true in the gospel. Jesus Christ, with all his goodness, is offered freely and sincerely to every soul. Though not all will receive him, he is given as a gift to all.

Too often, those who struggle with assurance feel like outsiders to the splendours of the New Testament. Like urban pedestrians on a cold winter night, we see others through the front windows of a restaurant. We witness the joy of those feasting at the tables; we see their happy faces and the steam rising from their dinner plates. We pass by the front door, smell the delicious aromas from within, and even hear snippets of cheerful conversation. But we do not think we ourselves are permitted to enter.

Yet when we come to see Christ as God's gift to us, when we embrace the gospel as God's promise to *us*, suddenly we are whisked indoors. We were meant to be here all along! We are able, at last, to see clearly that all the most beautiful promises are not just for others, but they are also for *us*. We find that Jesus came to give life abundantly to us (John 10:10). He laid down his life for *you* (John

---

[10] Thomas Boston, in Edward Fisher, *The Marrow of Modern Divinity* (Fearn, Ross-shire: Christian Focus, 2009), pp. 136-137.

10:11). He gives *me* eternal life, and nobody can snatch *me* out of his hand (John 10:28). Every gospel proposition is Jesus Christ saying to you and to me, 'This is what I promise to do for *you.*'

When we really come to grips with this, it will melt our heart, for it changes our view of God. When you see that God's promises are given not just to others, but also to you, then you will begin to see God not just as powerful, but also as beautiful. Believing those promises then becomes not just something one has to do, but also something one *wants* to do.

Christ is God's gift to the world for salvation. The free offer of the gospel is God's promise to all, which includes you and me. This precious truth is our third light to help us find certainty and dispel the fog of the valley of the shadow of doubt: *by its very nature, the gospel is God's promise to me.*

Theological Truth 4

BELIEVING GOD

Abraham believed God, and it was counted to him as righteousness.
(Romans 4:3)

By its very nature, the gospel is God's promise to you and to me. How then should we respond? 'The revelation of God is gospel, promise, the promise of forgiveness and salvation; but on our part nothing can match a promise except believing it: faith. Only by faith does a promise become our possession.'[11]

Thus far, our foundation for assurance of salvation rests on the character of God, the triumph of Jesus, and the free offer of the

---

[11] Herman Bavinck, *Reformed Dogmatics*, Vol. 1, *Prolegomena*, trans. John Vriend, ed. John Bolt (Grand Rapids: Baker Academic, 2003), p. 566.

gospel. To this base we must add two more layers which deal with the nature and efficacy of Christian faith.

What does it mean to have faith in Jesus Christ? In its most general sense, faith is *believing God*. The foundational text is Genesis 15:1-6:

> After these things the word of the Lord came to Abram in a vision: 'Fear not, Abram, I am your shield; your reward shall be very great.' But Abram said, 'O Lord God, what will you give me, for I continue childless, and the heir of my house is Eliezer of Damascus?' And Abram said, 'Behold, you have given me no offspring, and a member of my household will be my heir.' And behold, the word of the Lord came to him: 'This man shall not be your heir; your very own son shall be your heir.' And he brought him outside and said, 'Look toward heaven, and number the stars, if you are able to number them.' Then he said to him, 'So shall your offspring be.' And he believed the Lord, and he counted it to him as righteousness.

Citing this very passage in Romans 4:1-3, Paul underlines this simple essence of faith:

> What then shall we say was gained by Abraham, our forefather according to the flesh? For if Abraham was justified by works, he has something to boast about, but not before God. For what does the Scripture say? 'Abraham believed God, and it was counted to him as righteousness.'

Abraham did not just believe truth *about* God; he believed God *himself*. Faith is not a mere grasp of information, it is a relationship with a person. So Christian faith is not just knowledge about Christ, it is personal trust in Christ himself.

The answer to the eighty-sixth question of the *Westminster Shorter Catechism* defines faith in Jesus Christ as 'a saving grace, whereby we receive and rest upon him alone for salvation, as he is offered to us in the gospel.' But how can we 'receive and rest' upon a person who is not physically present? The Catechism points us toward the answer when it speaks of us receiving and resting on Jesus 'as he is offered to us in the gospel.' As we saw previously, the free offer of the gospel is God's promise to us. The key word here is *promise*.

Promises are the way we form a believing connection to another person. A promise is an extension of the one who makes it, a commitment of the promiser to do what is promised. To believe a promise is to take hold of the person who made it. What did Abraham believe? Abraham believed God would keep his promise: 'Look toward heaven, and number the stars, if you are able to number them … So shall your offspring be.'

Promises are the bridge between heaven and our hearts. Jesus Christ is in heaven, but his promises are here with us in his word. The gospel promise is his open hand of love. Though we cannot yet take hold of Christ's physical person, we may now take hold of his word of promise. In receiving his promise we receive him, for a promise may never be separated from the one who gives it.

Promises are the key to faith. John Calvin wrote,

> Here, indeed, is the chief hinge on which faith turns: that we do not regard the promises of mercy that God offers as true only outside ourselves, but not at all in us; rather that we make them ours by inwardly embracing them.[12]

What does it mean to embrace the gospel promises? The sixtieth question of the *Heidelberg Catechism* asks, 'How are you righteous before God?' Here is the answer:

---

[12] John Calvin, *Institutes of the Christian Religion*, ed. John T. McNeill, trans. Ford Lewis Battles, vols. 20-21 in The Library of Christian Classics (Louisville: Westminster John Knox, 1960), 3.2.16.

Only by true faith in Jesus Christ. Even though my conscience accuses me of having grievously sinned against all God's commandments, of never having kept any of them, and of still being inclined toward all evil, nevertheless, without any merit of my own, out of sheer grace, God grants and credits to me the perfect satisfaction, righteousness, and holiness of Christ, as if I had never sinned nor been a sinner, and as if I had been as perfectly obedient as Christ was obedient for me. – if only I accept this gift with a believing heart.

Notice how many times the Catechism uses the word 'my,' 'me,' or 'I'. Embracing the promises means receiving them as not just given to others, but as given to *me*. Thomas Boston underlines this point:

This act of faith is nothing else but to 'believe God' (1 John 5:10); 'to believe the Son' (John 3:36); 'to believe the report' concerning Christ (Isa. 53:1); or 'to believe the gospel' (Mark 1:15); not as devils believe the same, knowing Christ to be Jesus, a Saviour, but not their Saviour, but with an appropriating persuasion, or special application believing him to be our Saviour.[13]

Christian faith receives Christ as God's gift to *me*. It is believing all that he did, he did for *me*. It is believing Jesus will keep his gospel promises to *me*. In so doing, I rest my destiny in his hands.

How can I know if my faith is personal in this way? How can I distinguish true from counterfeit faith? True faith never separates the promise of life from the Lord who gives it. True faith receives not just Christ's *promises*, but also his *person*: 'But to all who did receive *him* …' (John 1:12). In resting on Christ's promises, I rest on *him*, welcoming him as my God and my friend. I do not just want to be saved *by* Jesus; I want to be *with* Jesus. I seek not just Christ's *cross*, but also his *kingdom*. I welcome not just his *power*, but also his

---

[13] Boston, in Fisher, *Marrow of Modern Divinity*, pp. 136-137.

presence. I desire not just his *salvation*, but also his *smile*. True faith *knows* there can be no heaven without Christ, and true faith *wants* no heaven but Christ's.

Our fourth light is this understanding of faith: Believing the promise unites us to the promiser.

Theological Truth 5

OUR STRONG BRANCH

No unbelief made him waver concerning the promise of God, but he grew strong in his faith as he gave glory to God, fully convinced that God was able to do what he had promised.
(Romans 4:20, 21)

Faith in Jesus Christ is necessary for salvation. 'Whoever believes in him is not condemned, but whoever does not believe is condemned already, because he has not believed in the name of the only Son of God' (John 3:18). We must really and personally believe in Jesus Christ. But how does faith save us? What happens when our faith is weak? Does weak faith endanger our salvation? The final layer in our foundation for assurance of salvation concerns the efficacy of faith.

It is at this very point – the necessity of belief – that many struggles with assurance find their crux. If faith is necessary for salvation, and believing is something I must do, then how can I ever know that I have done it right? This fear is understandable. With eternity in the balance, who should not be concerned about the integrity or quality of their faith? Yet at the same time, this fear is also based on a serious error. Exposing this error can go a long way toward helping us reach assurance. What do we mean?

When we worry about whether we are 'doing it right' with regard to our faith, we are treating faith, the act of *believing*, as though it were an act of *achieving* – a special work by which we earn our salvation. But this could not be further from the truth! Faith is not a work. Believing is not achieving. The apostle Paul clearly sets the two in contrast when he writes, 'For by grace you have been saved through faith. And this is not your own doing; it is the gift of God, not a result of works, so that no one may boast' (Eph. 2:8, 9). He expresses the same truth at greater length in his discussion of Abraham's faith, to which we have already referred in part:

> What then shall we say was gained by Abraham, our forefather according to the flesh? For if Abraham was justified by works, he has something to boast about, but not before God. For what does the Scripture say? 'Abraham believed God, and it was counted to him as righteousness.' Now to the one who works, his wages are not counted as a gift but as his due. And to the one who does not work but believes in him who justifies the ungodly, his faith is counted as righteousness … (Rom. 4:1-5).

Paul could not be clearer. Abraham's faith was not a work that earned justification, but rather he 'believed God,' the one who 'justifies the ungodly' and who 'counts righteousness apart from works' (Rom. 4:6).

This is tremendous news. But how can it be? How can faith be something we do, yet *not* be a work? It is at this very point that we must lean back on what we have already discovered about faith. Faith is not *persuading* Jesus to keep his promises. Faith is *believing* Jesus will keep his promises to me. Faith does not *achieve* my salvation. Faith *receives* my salvation in Christ. Faith rests not on its *own* ability or power. Rather, faith rests on the ability and power of *God*.

Continuing to draw on the story of Abraham, Paul underlines this point:

In hope he believed against hope, that he should become the father of many nations, as he had been told, 'So shall your offspring be.' He did not weaken in faith when he considered his own body, which was as good as dead (since he was about a hundred years old), or when he considered the barrenness of Sarah's womb. No unbelief made him waver concerning the promise of God, but he grew strong in his faith as he gave glory to God, fully convinced that God was able to do what he had promised. That is why his faith was 'counted to him as righteousness' (Rom. 4:18-22).

Abraham 'grew strong in his faith as he gave glory to God, fully convinced that God was able to do what he had promised.' Our faith finds all its hope not in its subject (I who believe), but in its object (Christ Jesus in whom I trust). Faith contributes nothing and receives everything. John Murray wrote:

It is to be remembered that the efficacy of faith does not reside in itself. Faith is not something that merits the favour of God. All the efficacy unto salvation resides in the Saviour. As one has aptly and truly stated the case, it is not faith that saves but faith in Jesus Christ; strictly speaking, it is not even faith in Christ that saves but Christ that saves through faith … The specific character of faith is that it looks away from itself and finds its whole interest and object in Christ.[14]

Because our faith is based on Christ's promises rather than our performance, it remains effective even when it is weak. Tim Keller offers a vivid illustration:

Imagine you are on a high cliff and you lose your footing and begin to fall. Just beside you as you fall is a branch sticking out of the very edge of the cliff. It is your only hope and it is more than strong enough to support your weight. How can it save

---

[14] Murray, *Redemption Accomplished and Applied*, p. 113.

you? If your mind is filled with intellectual certainty that the branch can support you, but you don't actually reach out and grab it, you are lost. If your mind is instead filled with doubts and uncertainty that the branch can hold you, but you reach out and grab it anyway, you will be saved. Why? It is not the strength of your faith but the object of your faith that actually saves you. Strong faith in a weak branch is fatally inferior to weak faith in a strong branch.[15]

This is the essential point: We are not saved by the quality of our convictions *about* Christ, but only by the reality of our connection to Christ.[16] We are saved not by *how well*, but only by *whom* we trust.

This reality of how faith saves is our fifth light. No matter how little your knowledge or how many your doubts, no matter how weak your faith, Christ *is* strong enough to uphold you. Because he is our strong branch, *it is not how much or how well you believe, but only whom you trust that saves you.*

---

[15] Timothy Keller, *The Reason for God: Belief in an Age of Skepticism* (New York: Dutton, 2008), p. 232.

[16] Reinforcing this point is the fact that faith itself 'is not your own doing; it is the gift of God,' (Eph. 2:8). Faith is not self-created; it is implanted in our hearts by the Holy Spirit when God the Father draws us to Christ (Titus 3:5, John 6:44). This life-giving connection is God's gift. Will he let it fail? Never! 'By God's power [we] are being guarded through faith for a salvation ready to be revealed in the last time,' (1 Pet. 1:5).

Practical Step 1

PROVING FAITH LIVES

How then will they call on him in whom they have not believed?
(Romans 10:13)

Having laid a foundation for the assurance of our salvation in the theological truths of who God is, what Christ accomplished, the promise of the gospel, and the operation of faith, we are now in a position to implement a few practical counter-measures.

In order to prevent or defeat perpetual doubts about the reality of our faith, we must find a way to break the endless cycle of uncertainty. There is a proper time and place for spiritual self-examination. But there is also such a thing as morbid introspection: an unhealthy inability to stop thinking about oneself.[17] It is right and proper to pause occasionally in order to take stock of what and how one believes. But afterward, there comes the call for decisive activity. We have done the former. It is now time for the latter. How do we proceed?

God commands you and I to believe *right now*. 'And this is his commandment, that we believe in the name of his Son Jesus Christ' (1 John 3:23). Reflecting on this, Edward Fisher comments,

> 'Wherefore, you having so good a warrant as God's command, and so great an encouragement as his promise, do your duty; and by the doing thereof you may put it [your believing] out of question, and be sure that you are also one of God's elect.'[18]

The first practical step, then, is to *prove faith's existence by its exercise*. Instead of endlessly *examining* your faith, *exercise* it! A wise

---

[17] I am indebted to D. Martyn Lloyd-Jones for this definition.
[18] Edward Fisher, *Marrow of Modern Divinity*, p. 145.

older minister once said to me, 'What I tell people who are unsure is: *just trust him now*.' Prove your faith lives. But how do you do this? The best way to prove you are alive is to breathe. In the same way, the best way to prove your faith lives is to make it breathe. How does faith breathe? 'Just as the first sign of life in an infant when born into the world, is the act of breathing, so the first act of men and women when they are born again, is *praying*.'[19] David writes, 'Trust in him at all times, O people; pour out your heart before him; God is a refuge for us' (Psa. 62:8).

Faith breathes by prayer. Prayer vocalizes faith. Note how the apostle Paul sets the two in parallel:

> For the Scripture says, 'Everyone who believes in him will not be put to shame.' For there is no distinction between Jew and Greek; for the same Lord is Lord of all, bestowing his riches on all who call on him. For 'everyone who calls on the name of the Lord will be saved' (Rom. 10:11-13).

In vocalizing faith, there are no magic words. Our Lord is not interested in a rehearsed speech, but looks for a broken and contrite heart (Psa. 51:17). We see this movingly illustrated in the parable of the prodigal son (Luke 15:11-32). When he came to his senses, the prodigal son prepared a fine and accurate statement of repentance (verses 18, 19). Yet when he arrived back home, his father would not allow him to finish his carefully rehearsed speech (verses 21, 22). Why not? Because what mattered was not the *form of the words*, but rather the *honesty of the heart* from which the words flowed.

Paul asks, 'How then will they call on him in whom they have not believed?' (Rom. 10:14). How indeed! If you sincerely pray to him, you must believe in him. *The exercise of sincere prayer proves the existence of true faith.*

[19] J. C Ryle, *Practical Religion* (Edinburgh: Banner of Truth Trust, 2013), p. 61.

Practical Step 2

PROVING YOUR HEART

Blessed are those who hunger and thirst for righteousness,
for they shall be satisfied.
(Matthew 5:6)

The exercise of sincere prayer proves the existence of true faith. Yet as soon as we mention sincerity, the sensitive heart may tremble. 'The heart is deceitful above all things, and desperately sick; who can understand it?' (Jer. 17:9). The human capacity for self-deception is almost boundless. How can we know whether we are truly sincere? *By examining our desires.*

The psalmist expressed his longing for the Lord: 'Whom have I in heaven but you? And there is nothing on earth that I desire besides you,' (Psa. 73:25). Paul wrote movingly of his willingness to 'count everything as loss because of the surpassing worth of knowing Christ Jesus my Lord' (Phil. 3:8). And our Lord Jesus blessed 'those who hunger and thirst for righteousness, for they shall be satisfied,' (Matt. 5:6).

Do you hunger and thirst for righteousness? Though you may at times yet experience sinful desires, do you desire Jesus more than anything else? *This is a certain mark of regeneration*:

> For those who live according to the flesh set their minds on the things of the flesh, but those who live according to the Spirit set their minds on the things of the Spirit. For to set the mind on the flesh is death, but to set the mind on the Spirit is life and peace. For the mind that is set on the flesh is hostile to God, for it does not submit to God's law; indeed, it cannot. Those who are in the flesh cannot please God. You, however, are not in the flesh but in the Spirit, if in fact the Spirit of God dwells in you.

Anyone who does not have the Spirit of Christ does not belong to him. But if Christ is in you, although the body is dead because of sin, the Spirit is life because of righteousness (Rom. 8:5-10).

Recall our very first theological truth about believing God's verdict even when we do not feel it. Now apply the logic of this passage to your heart. If you desire God, then you are clearly not hostile to him, and therefore, you are *not* one whose mind is set on the things of the flesh. Rather, if you desire Christ, you *must* be one of those who have set their minds on the things of the Spirit, who 'live according to the Spirit,' who 'have the Spirit of Christ.' Therefore, 'Christ is in you.' Consider a second passage:

> Now we have received not the spirit of the world, but the Spirit who is from God, that we might understand the things freely given us by God. And we impart this in words not taught by human wisdom but taught by the Spirit, interpreting spiritual truths to those who are spiritual. The natural person does not accept the things of the Spirit of God, for they are folly to him, and he is not able to understand them because they are spiritually discerned (1 Cor. 2:12-14).

Again, apply the logic. If you desire Christ, then you 'understand the things freely given us by God' and are accepting the things of God. Therefore, you must no longer be a 'natural person.'

The significance of our desires in ascertaining the condition of our hearts is confirmed in the *Westminster Larger Catechism*. Question 172 asks, 'May one who doubteth of his being in Christ, or of his due preparation, come to the Lord's Supper?' Here is the answer:

> One who doubteth of his being in Christ, or of his due preparation to the sacrament of the Lord's supper, may have true interest in Christ, though he be not yet assured thereof; and in God's account hath it, if he be duly affected with the apprehension of

the want of it, and unfeignedly desires to be found in Christ, and to depart from iniquity: in which case (because promises are made, and this sacrament is appointed, for the relief even of weak and doubting Christians) he is to bewail his unbelief, and labour to have his doubts resolved; and, so doing, he may and ought to come to the Lord's supper, that he may be further strengthened.

Here is solid pastoral wisdom. One who doubts whether he has salvation in Christ 'in God's account hath it' if he understands what it would mean to be eternally lost and 'unfeignedly desires to be found in Christ, and depart from iniquity.' Our heart's *desires*, therefore, are true indicators of our heart's *direction*. Thus the second practical step in overcoming doubts is to *prove our sincerity by examining our desires.*

Practical Step 3

PROVING THE REALITY BY THE REMEDY

Thomas answered him, 'My Lord and my God!'
(John 20:28)

We can prove faith's existence by its exercise. We can prove our sincerity by examining our desires. We can do all this, and yet still find that doubts persist. Why does this happen?

God's work in us – our sanctification – is not an event, but a process. The answer to the thirty-fifth question of the *Westminster Shorter Catechism* reminds us that 'sanctification is the work of God's free grace, whereby we are renewed in the whole man after the image of God, and are enabled more and more to die unto sin, and live unto righteousness.' We are renewed 'more and more,' but not all at once. So we should expect both progress and setbacks in our struggle for assurance just as we see both progress and setbacks in our living how God desires. Nevertheless, there is one final practical step that we may implement. We may *prove the reality by the remedy*. That is, we may prove the reality of our faith by the remedy we seek for its deficiency.

At the cross, our Lord Jesus turned the enemy's darkest weapon into the very means by which the enemy was vanquished. Crucifixion was supposed to destroy the Son of God. Instead, it was *through crucifixion* that Christ broke the power of darkness forever: 'that through death he might destroy the one who has the power of death, that is, the devil, and deliver all those who through fear of death were subject to lifelong slavery' (Heb. 2:14-15). What if we could do the same thing with our doubts?

To prove the reality by the remedy means *to use every instance of doubt as an opportunity to destroy doubt*. When you find yourself wrestling with a recurring doubt or fear, do not *obsess* about it. Rather, *confess* it! Do not let these things push you *away* from Christ. Let them propel you toward him. Jesus died to rescue you *even from disbelief*. Did he cast out Thomas? No, he invited him to believe:

> Now Thomas, one of the twelve, called the Twin, was not with them when Jesus came. So the other disciples told him, 'We have seen the Lord.' But he said to them, 'Unless I see in his hands the mark of the nails, and place my finger into the mark of the nails, and place my hand into his side, I will never believe.' Eight days later, his disciples were inside again, and Thomas was with them. Although the doors were locked, Jesus came and stood among them and said, 'Peace be with you.' Then he said to Thomas, 'Put your finger here, and see my hands; and put out your hand, and place it in my side. Do not disbelieve, but believe.' Thomas answered him, 'My Lord and my God!' (John 20:24-28).

The world, the flesh, and the devil love to whisper doubts through the windows of a sensitive soul. A heart that is acquainted with its own darkness may often tremble in the shadow of the question, 'What if I am self-deceived?' But what if we could turn this fear against itself?

What if, from now on, we simply *give every question to Jesus*? Let us gather up, right now, all our uncertainties and place them into the hands that hung the stars, the hands that hung on the cross, the hands extended to us in the gospel promises, the hands of the one who promised never to let us go. Ask yourself, 'What do I fear will separate me from Christ?' Then take the answer and turn it into a prayer: 'Lord Jesus, save me, even from *this*.' If we confess it *to* Christ, how can it ever separate us *from* him? 'If we confess our sins, he is faithful and just to forgive us our sins and to cleanse us from all unrighteousness' (1 John 1:9).

When we confess our fears, doubt becomes its own undoing, for to *call* to Jesus is to *believe* in him (Rom. 10:11-14), to *believe* in him is *come* to him (John 7:37-38), and to *come* to him is to *belong* to him forever (John 6:37). *When our faith is weak, we prove its reality by the remedy we seek.*

Conclusion

IN THE HANDS OF JESUS

Into your hand I commit my spirit;
you have redeemed me, O Lord, faithful God.
(Psalm 31:5)

We may prove that our faith lives. We may prove that our hearts are sincere. We may even disarm our doubts by giving them directly into the hands of Jesus. We may do all this day by day, and still find that our hearts are distressingly restless.

The roots of restlessness will vary. Habit and temperament weave strange cobwebs in the soul, and stress is often a spider in the shadows. No two struggles are exactly the same. But there is one thing that is common to all searches for certainty in our Christian experience: *the solution*. Whatever the symptoms of our restlessness, the final answer is ultimately the same for each of us: we must rest in Christ – and in Christ *alone*. Augustine's memorable prayer is true for every soul, 'You have made us for yourself, and our heart is restless until it rests in you.'[20]

Yet what if resting is the problem? If faith involves resting and my heart is restless, I may again begin to doubt whether my faith is real after all. I know that I am saved not by *how well*, but in *whom*, I trust, and every day I sincerely strive to give every question to Jesus. But, if despite all this I still feel restless, could my restlessness be a sign that I am yet self-deceived?

Such restlessness can make us feel like we are back at square one. It can convince us that we will never actually find certainty in our spiritual experience. Despite all that I have learned over the years and sought to communicate in the previous pages, this is still a place where I frequently find myself stuck. But there is a way out of this final doubt too. Look again at the finished work of Jesus, and you will see that his perfect life includes a *perfect faith*:

> In the days of his flesh, Jesus offered up prayers and supplications, with loud cries and tears, to him who was able to save him from death, and he was heard because of his reverence. Although he was a son, he learned obedience through what he suffered. And being made perfect, he became the source of eternal salvation to all who obey him, being designated by God a high priest after the order of Melchizedek (Heb. 5:7-10).

[20] Augustine, *Confessions*, tr. Henry Chadwick (Oxford: OUP, 1998), p. 3.

Later in the same letter, Jesus is called 'the founder and perfecter of our faith,' (Heb. 12:2). Commenting on this, Geerhardus Vos writes:

> Faith ... through which a guilty sinner becomes just in the sight of God, our Lord could not exercise, because he was sinless. But the faith that is an assurance of things hoped for and a proving of things not seen had a large place in his experience.[21]

What does it mean to say that Jesus had faith? Remember what faith means: to embrace God's promises personally. In our case, the promise is for *redemption*: that we will be raised to life *instead* of dying for our sins. In the case of Jesus, however, the promise was for *vindication*: that he would be raised to life *after* dying for our sins. Being sinless, Jesus had no need of a promise of forgiveness. But in dying for sinners, Jesus believed the promise of resurrection for the Messiah (Psa. 16:10; 22:22-31; Isa. 53:10-12). So there is a difference between what Jesus believed and what we believe. But there is no difference in *whom* we believe. Jesus believed God, so do we (Rom. 4:3).

What does this mean for us? As we saw earlier, the life of Christ was an act of double substitution (2 Cor. 5:21). *All* that Jesus did, he did *for us*. And these passages from Hebrews show us that Jesus was not just perfect for us in his thoughts, words, and deeds. He was also perfect for us in his *faith*. Even at death, his faith was flawless:

'Father, into your hands I commit my spirit!' (Luke 23:46).

In these precious words, we have a way out of the final doubt. Because Jesus trusted God perfectly, because his life includes a per- fect faith, Jesus has made atonement *even for the flaws in our faith*. The work of Christ applies *even to our act of believing*. All of our restlessness is clothed in his perfect confidence. In the hands of Christ I am saved from all the doubts in my soul, even the doubts in my faith.

---

[21] Geerhardus Vos, *Grace and Glory* (Edinburgh: Banner of Truth Trust, 1994), p. 104.

Most Christians have been taught that the blood and righteousness of Jesus cover the sins and failures in our *life*. What we need to know now, and remember tomorrow, is that our Lord's perfection also covers the sins and failures in our *faith*: 'The blood of Jesus his Son cleanses us from *all* sin,' (1 John 1:7). There is nothing God requires that Christ does not supply; we are saved *by grace* (Eph. 2:8, 9).

The moment we commit our spirits into the hands of Jesus, he proclaims a tremendous promise over even the feeblest faith: 'I give them eternal life, and they will never perish, and no one will snatch them out of my hand' (John 10:28). We see this beautifully illustrated in the Gospel account of Peter walking on the water toward Jesus:

> In the fourth watch of the night he came to them, walking on the sea. But when the disciples saw him walking on the sea, they were terrified, and said, 'It is a ghost!' and they cried out in fear. But immediately Jesus spoke to them, saying, 'Take heart; it is I. Do not be afraid.'
>
> And Peter answered him, 'Lord, if it is you, command me to come to you on the water.' He said, 'Come.' So Peter got out of the boat and walked on the water and came to Jesus. But when he saw the wind, he was afraid, and beginning to sink he cried out, 'Lord, save me.' Jesus immediately reached out his hand and took hold of him, saying to him, 'O you of little faith, why did you doubt?' (Matt. 14:25-31).

Jesus takes the flawed-in-faith safely in hand. He does not let us sink. He holds our sinking hearts in his strong, sure hands. Safe within this ark our faith shall indeed overcome the world (1 John 5:4). The simple, wonderful reality is this: even the imperfections of our faith cannot separate us from the love of Christ. 'I am sure that neither death nor life, nor angels nor rulers, nor things present nor things to come, nor powers, nor height nor depth, nor anything else in all creation, will be able to separate us from the love of God in Christ Jesus our Lord' (Rom. 8:38, 39).

Our third practical step instructed us to prove the reality of our faith by the remedy we seek for its weakness, to turn our doubts into their own undoing by giving them directly to Jesus. To escape the valley of the shadow of doubt once and for all, we must apply this remedy to *even the imperfections of our faith.*

To do this, we follow our Lord's own example. As he hung dying on the cross, as the darkness closed in on him both physically and spiritually, as he faced the most horrible uncertainty ever experienced – 'My God, my God, why have you forsaken me?' (Mark 15:34) – how did our Saviour respond? He took up the words of faith from Psalm 31:5: 'Into your hand I commit my spirit; you have redeemed me, O Lord, faithful God.' He took these words, he made them his own: 'Father, into your hands I commit my spirit!' (Luke 23:46). Since this was the perfect response of faith to Christ's ultimate uncertainty, then it must also be the perfect response of faith to our every lesser uncertainty. Knowing these words were acceptable to the Father from Jesus in his valley of deepest darkness, we can be confident that they will be acceptable to Jesus from us as we pass through the lesser valleys of our doubts and fears: 'Jesus, into your hands I commit my spirit and my imperfect faith.'

It really is as simple as this. Although these words may not be an instant cure, they are the perfect way to place everything where it needs to be. With these words I take his promises as my resting place, put my heart in his hands, and walk toward the dawn of spiritual certainty.

BOOKLETS IN THIS SERIES

Abortion *Peter Barnes*

The Agency that Transformed a Nation *J. C. Ryle*

The Authentic Gospel *Jeffrey E. Wilson*

Behind a Frowning Providence *John J. Murray*

The Bleeding of the Evangelical Church *David Wells*

Burial or Cremation? Does It Matter? *Donald Howard*

A Call to Prayer *J. C. Ryle*

Can We Know God? *Maurice Roberts*

The Carnal Christian *Ernest Reisinger*

The Christian Sabbath *Terry L. Johnson*

Christians Grieve Too *Donald Howard*

Coming to Faith in Christ *John Benton*

The Cross: the Pulpit of God's Love *Iain H. Murray*

The Cross: the Vindication of God *D. M. Lloyd-Jones*

A Defence of Calvinism *C. H. Spurgeon*

Evangelistic Calvinism *John Benton*

Finding Peace with God *Maurice J. Roberts*

The Five Points of Calvinism *W. J. Seaton*

The Free Offer of the Gospel *John Murray*

Healthy Christian Growth *Sinclair B. Ferguson*

Her Husband's Crown *Sara Leone*

Holiness *Joel R. Beeke*

The Incomparable Book *W. J. McDowell*

The Invitation System *Iain H. Murray*

Jesus Christ and Him Crucified *D. M. Lloyd-Jones*

A Life of Principled Obedience *A. N. Martin*

Living the Christian Life *A. N. Martin*

Power in the Pulpit *Henry C. Fish*

The Practical Implications of Calvinism *A. N. Martin*

Preaching that Gets Through *Stuart Olyott*

Preaching: The Centrality of Scripture *R. Albert Mohler*
Precious Promises *Joseph Alleine*
The Priority of Preaching *John Cheeseman*
The Psalter — The Only Hymnal? *Iain H. Murray*
Read Any Good Books? *Sinclair B. Ferguson*
Reading the Bible *Geoffrey Thomas*
Reading the Bible and Praying in Public *Stuart Olyott*
Rest in God *Iain H. Murray*
Shorter Catechism with Scripture Proofs *Westminster Divines*
Simplicity in Preaching *J. C. Ryle*
Study Guide for The Mortification of Sin *Rob Edwards*
Study Guide for The Promise of the Future *Cornelis P. Venema*
The Unresolved Controversy *Iain H. Murray*
Victory: The Work of the Spirit *Pieter Potgieter*
Walking Toward the Dawn *Jeremiah W. Montgomery*
Welcome to the Library *Sinclair B. Ferguson*
What Is the Reformed Faith? *J. R. de Witt*
What's Wrong with Preaching Today? *A. N. Martin*
Whom Shall I Marry? *Andrew Swanson*
Why Read Church History? *J. Philip Arthur*
Wisdom Everywhere *Sinclair B. Ferguson*
Worship *J. C. Ryle*

BANNER *of* **TRUTH**

The Banner of Truth Trust originated in 1957 in London. The founders believed that much of the best literature of historic Christianity had been allowed to fall into oblivion and that, under God, its recovery could well lead not only to a strengthening of the church, but to true revival.

Interdenominational in vision, this publishing work is now international, and our lists include a number of contemporary authors, together with classics from the past. The translation of these books into many languages is encouraged.

A monthly magazine, *The Banner of Truth*, is also published, and further information about this, and all our other publications, may be found on our website, banneroftruth.org, or by contacting the offices below:

Head Office:
3 Murrayfield Road
Edinburgh
EH12 6EL
United Kingdom
Email: info@banneroftruth.co.uk

North America Office:
PO Box 621
Carlisle, PA 17013
United States of America
Email: info@banneroftruth.org